Dividend Investing

Explained

In Less Than 45 Pages

A Guide for New Investors

Lori O'Dette-Robinson, M.S., CISSP

Note:

Every possible attempt has been made to verify that the information provided in this book is both true and accurate at the time and date of publication. Any changes to the reference or resource URLs provided are the sole responsibility of the resource website owner. Neither the publisher nor author assume any liability for any injury and/or damage or loss to a person or property as a matter of products liability, negligence or otherwise, or from any use or operation of any methods, products, instructions, or ideas contained in the material herein.

DEDICATION

This book is dedicated to my husband, family, and friends.

This book is also dedicated to all of the people who want to gain both control over their finances and enough knowledge to make some or all decisions concerning their investments without having to pay high fees.

ACKNOWLEDGEMENTS

I would like to thank the honest reviews, corrections, and editing tips received from Pat, Lynne & John, Scott, Carol, and Terri.

TABLE OF CONTENTS

PREFACE

This book was written to provide the basic knowledge and tools necessary for the average person to open an account with a brokerage firm, whether in person or online, with the intent purpose to invest in the stock market. This book will provide information specific to understanding the difference between dividend paying stocks and non-dividend paying stocks.

This book is also intentionally written to stay under 50 pages. It is my experience that many readers are very busy and do not always have the time to read a 300-400 page average sized guide book. My intention is to provide a good base of knowledge and also provide additional knowledge resources that are free online.

Just to clarify, I am not a Financial Consultant or Planner. I am the average person who has invested in the stock market for over 10 years. I am an Information Security Consultant with a Masters Degree. I use the same research and analysis skills that I have developed and honed over the last 19 years for Information Technology to research and analyze the American stock market, economy, and retirement planning options. With that said, I am not a paid contributor to any financial news outlets. I am also not receiving any affiliate or kickback fees for recommending any financial products, services, or methods included in this book.

I hope you enjoy this book and are able to take away the basic information related to the stock market and brokerage firms that you will need when communicating with financial professionals.

All suggestions and recommendations provided in this book are unbiased. If you have any questions, comments, or would like pointers to additional resource information not provided here – please use the question submission form located on the financial page of my website: www.WebLori.com.

CHAPTER 1

INTRODUCTION TO INVESTING

Brief History Lesson (yawn here if you like)

I would like to start with a little history of the stock market. According to MONEY-ZINE™ (www.money-zine.com,2013), the history of the stock market began in 1698 with the creation of the London Stock Exchange. The New York Stock Exchange (NYSE) was formed in 1792 and the American Stock Exchange (AMEX) in 1849. The Bombay stock exchange (Mumbai, India) is traced back to 1875. Lastly, the National Association of Securities Dealers Automated Quotation (NASDAQ) appeared on the scene in 1971. (This can be boring stuff unless you really like history).

Now, all of the stocks that are traded in America are regulated by the Security and Exchange Commission (SEC), which was founded in response to the Stock Market Crash of 1929. The Securities Act of 1933 and the Securities and Exchange Act of 1934 were passed into law by Congress to enforce securities laws passed by Congress. So, Congress created two new laws to enforce future laws governing securities activities in the United States. (I am trying desperately NOT to add a personal comment here regarding Congress' perceived efficient behavior compared to our current Congress' perceived behavior).

The NYSE originated with the brokers gathering by the Buttonwood tree located next to Wall Street. It is believed to have first been named "de Waal Straat" by the Dutch settlers. New York was originally settled as New Amsterdam (Nieuw Amsterdam) between 1609 and 1625.

It was later named after the Duke of York (future James II of England) in 1655 when the English took control. Our current Wall Street was defined using the line from the original stockade built to fortify the early settlement located at the tip of Manhattan. The fortification was believed to be required to protect the settlers from both the English and the Native American Indians. (And you think New Yorkers are paranoid now? The Dutch settlers had them beat!).

Back to the stock market - in the early days of the New York exchanges, a company had to be able to offer at least 100 shares in order to be listed on the exchange. If the company could not offer that many shares, they depended on the curb brokers. These were brokers who stood outside the NYSE on the street and traded shares at the curbside. This practice continued for about 150 years until the curb exchange became the AMEX in 1953.

The Stock Exchange

You may be asking, "What exactly is a stock exchange?" According to Wikipedia (http://en.wikipedia.org/wiki/Stock_exchange, 2013), a stock exchange can be defined as:

> "a form of exchange which provides services for stock brokers and traders to trade stocks, bonds, and other securities. Stock exchanges also provide facilities for issue and redemption of securities and other financial instruments, and capital events including the payment of income and dividends. Securities traded on a stock exchange include shares issued by companies, unit trusts, derivatives, pooled investment products and bonds."

According to the definition of a stock exchange listed above, it appears that in order for someone to purchase shares (or other forms of securities) issued by companies, that person must somehow purchase them through an exchange. In order for you, the individual investor, to be able to purchase shares on the stock exchange, you must engage a licensed and regulated stock broker.

This stock broker is normally associated with a brokerage firm and can purchase the stocks shares on your behalf for a fee. We will discuss brokerage firms in more detail in chapter 2 (Stock Market and Brokerage Firms).

Stock Shares

So what exactly are stock shares? Briefly, an incorporated business can issue shares to be offered to the public for purchase or for sale (trade). The total value of the stock shares a company issues is supposed to be equal to the equity, or value of the ownership interest, from the company balance sheet. There are normally two categories of shares, common and preferred.

Common share owners have voting rights. Preferred share owners do not always have voting rights, but do normally receive dividends on the shares before the common share owners can receive theirs. For this book we will be focusing on dividend paying stock and common shares. As you may have surmised, not all stock shares pay dividends.

Keep in mind that a company can either reinvest their profits into the growth of the company, or they can distribute a portion of those profits back to the share holders in the form of a dividend or other distribution, or they can do both. Growth stocks normally do not return profits back to the share holders; they use the profits to grow the company, thereby increasing the value of the stock shares. This process normally works with the exception that they may have too much debt, or the markets are being negatively affected by the current state of the economy.

Why Invest?

The most common answer to that question is to grow your money. Making an investment in general terms normally involves turning over something you value with the expectation that the value of that item will grow or provide benefits for you over time. An example could be the time and money needed to acquire a college degree. You already know that the expectation of the college graduate is the high potential of securing a good paying job in their elected field. So the college graduate invests both time and money to achieve the return potential of the good job. That job would then provide enough pay to reimburse them for the previous time and money spent (tuition loans).

For financial investing, it also takes your time and money. The expectation here is that your money, invested wisely, will increase over time. The more time the investment has to grow, the larger it should become. Your investment can grow either by an increase in stock share value, or by the reinvestment of received dividends. I use the word "should" in the previous sentence as this is not always the outcome of an investment. Your invested time could also include the time you spend on educating yourself to better understand your investment, your strategy, and when to make changes.

Financial Consultants, Advisors, and Planners

Do you need a financial consultant, advisor, or planner? This is a good question. The strategy you choose to manage your financial investments may or may not involve this level of professional help. To make this book easier to read, we will call all of these people "financial professionals". You may only choose to engage a broker when you want to buy or sell stock shares or funds. The financial professional can also provide the broker service, or they will have access to a broker for you.

Sometimes these financial professionals get a bad reputation. People like us see them with expensive cars, big offices, and large houses. We immediately assume that they get all of their money from the fees they charge us for the products and services they sell us. This may be true in some cases, but I also want to remind you that the apparent wealth and success of the financial professional may also be a sign that they actually do know how to invest and grow money, and they are benefiting from their own personal investments.

How can you tell one from the other? How do we know which one is only interested in your fees, not the growth of your money? You may need to conduct a little research on the fee structure they charge for the products and services they offer. You may want to also conduct a little interview with the professional to make sure they are both registered with and comply with the rules and regulations governed by the Financial Industry Regulatory Authority (www.FINRA.org). FINRA is the independent regulator for all securities firms in the United States. They are dedicated to protect us, the investor, and the integrity of the stock markets. They also provide free learning resources on their website for individual investors like you and me. I will discuss choosing the right financial professional more in chapter 4 (Account Management).

Risk Tolerance

The last thing I want to introduce in this chapter is the idea of risk tolerance. This involves identifying how much risk you are willing to take when choosing the stocks to invest in. I have been through several risk tolerance questionnaires. They are designed to ask a series of questions to help identify our level of tolerance to risk. If you do not know your current level of tolerance, it may be helpful for you to take one of these questionnaires. I searched online for a free questionnaire to recommend, and located dozens. You can get a questionnaire (or survey) from your local financial professional, or you can go online (Rutgers University of New Jersey has one here: http://njaes.rutgers.edu/money/riskquiz/). You can find others by searching the internet using the following keyword patterns:

Risk tolerance questionnaire

Risk tolerance survey

Risk tolerance quiz

It would also benefit you to know your spouse's risk tolerance as well. This will help to ensure that your investment strategy will not stress out your significant other. Also keep in mind that as we get older and more experienced, our risk tolerance level may change. It may be prudent to take the questionnaire every few years to determine if your tolerance has changed and how to modify your investment strategy accordingly. Your financial professional may use the results from your questionnaire or survey and add them to your demographic information. Your age can dictate to them when to scale back on risk.

The older you get, the less risk you want to take. The idea behind this is to protect your retirement portfolio from risk the closer you are to actually needing it. If you are 20-30 years old, you have more **TIME** to recover your investment in the event of an economic recession. With this theory, you can take more risk in your investments. As we have learned from the recent recession that started in 2007, but came to a full head in 2010, it can take several years for the economy to recover. We are actually still trying to recover and it is 2013!

CHAPTER 2

STOCK MARKET AND BROKERAGE FIRMS

In this chapter, we will go into a little more detail about the stock exchange and brokerage firms. We already know that the stock exchange is where the stock shares issued by member companies are traded. By traded, I mean bought or sold by investors. We also know that in order for an investor to buy or sell a stock share, we need to engage a stock broker to conduct the transaction for us.

A brokerage firm is a financial institution that provides more than just the stock broker service, it also provides other services and products including financial professionals for consulting, advising, and planning. They have access to sell you other types of financial products as well. If the firm is not authorized to offer certain products, they can partner with other financial institutions that are. The products consist of an array of options for you to invest your money in. They can consist of annuities, certificates of deposit (CD), standard savings or college savings accounts, municipal or government bonds, treasuries, and individual stocks or groups of stocks sold together in a fund.

These firms can also manage your account if you do not choose to receive your stock shares in paper form, rather store them electronically. I have had both forms, and I prefer electronic now as I have had time to build confidence with the online account stability. When I did own paper stock share certificates, I always stored them in my local bank safe deposit box. The paper stock certificate is on the way out, so you will want to consider an online account for electronic storage.

Appendix A (Useful Online Resources) has three internet links for you to use to review the top brokerage firms. It is important that you hear what others are saying concerning the products and services these firms offer. You will also find information regarding any complaints, legal actions, and standard fees the firms charge for their services. Most of the fee information can also be located on each firm's website or by calling their customer service. I will talk more about this in chapter 4.

So far we have discussed a little of the history and the purpose of the stock exchange and an overview on brokerage firms, now we will discuss the stock market. A market is commonly thought of as a place to shop for various goods. It can include different shops and vendors. The stock market is very similar to this idea. It has different markets within the market itself. It is divided into nine "sectors" which are further sub-divided into multiple "industries", which are also further sub-divided into multiple stock "types". Does this sound complex? It actually is not that hard to understand when you see a few examples.

> **Example 1:** Let's say you are driving through Texas and see all of those oil derricks pumping crude oil to the surface. You then wonder "can I invest in the companies that own oil derricks?" The answer is yes, you can. They are found in this market:
>> Sector = Basic Materials (or Energy), Industry = Oil & Gas Drilling and Exploration, Type = Hard Asset.

> **Example 2:** You are now going to the local discount retail store to buy batteries, cat food, and a bunch of bananas. As you park your car, you wonder if you can find the market that this retailer falls under:
>> Sector = Consumer Goods, Industry = Discount Stores, Type = Aggressive Growth.

Example 3: You are reviewing your latest cell phone bill and are alarmed at the balance due. You start wondering why the phone company needs to charge you all these fees and why can't you own shares of this obviously profitable company:

> Sector = Communication Services, Industry = Telecommunications, Type = High Yield.

Example 4: Your need some quick cash and you pull into the ATM lane at your local bank. While you are waiting on that guy in front of you who is trying to remember his PIN, you wonder if your bank is listed on the stock market too:

> Sector = Financial Services, Industry = Banks – Regional-US, Type = Cyclical.

Example 5: You are shopping for a new car and see all of the different makes and models listed for sale in the Sunday newspaper. You remember reading that most of the car manufacturers received some kind of bailout during the recent recession, but they are now on the financial mend. You are wondering how much the share cost is now for the different automakers:

> Sector = Consumer Cyclical, Industry = Auto Manufacturers, Type = Cyclical.

Example 6: You are reviewing your monthly budget and examine your natural gas bill. You wonder what the current stock share price is for this public utility company:

> Sector = Utilities, Industry = Utilities – Regulated Gas, Type = Slow Growth.

If you are still following along, I hope you can see the basic breakdown of the structure of the markets. This information will come in handy when you are deciding on your investing strategy. You may have heard the term "diversify" before. This means to have a healthy mixture of stocks in more than one sector. The belief behind this is that owning a diversified mixture of stock from different sectors helps to lower the overall risk of your total investment, also known as a stock portfolio. We will discuss this further in chapter 5 (Set Goals, Make a Plan).

Here is a tip: if you want to see an example of a well diversified portfolio, just look at a couple of the more popular dividend based mutual funds. You can normally locate the top 10 or 20 stocks held by these funds and the percentage of each stock either on one of the stock market monitoring sites I provide in Appendix A, or on that mutual fund owner's website. This information is public knowledge.

CHAPTER 3

TERMS YOU NEED TO KNOW

There are literally hundreds of financial terms that you may run into during your personal financial planning. The learning curve related to those may seem overwhelming, but in reality you may never need to learn a majority of them. Appendix A provides internet links to three popular financial dictionaries. You can check those for terms as you continue your self-education.

For the sake of dividend investing, I am providing a definition for a few terms that you will need to understand to be able to effectively talk to a financial planner, consultant, or stock broker. Your need to understand these terms will be shown in chapter 5.

One of the first things you will need to know is what type of account you want to open to manage your investments. You may require more than one type of account, depending on your needs. Here are the 4 most common types of accounts:

Brokerage Account – this is the account that you will use to manage your stock related investments. This type of account can be used for either a retirement or non retirement related investment.

College Savings Account – this type of account is commonly restricted for use only with college related expenses, such as tuition and books. Some allow food and lodging expenses also. Most common are 529 or Coverdell plans.

Individual Retirement Account – this type of account is normally funded by you as an additional retirement savings vehicle. This is in addition to any retirement pension or 401k type plan your employer may offer. The federal government sets strict rules as to the amount you can contribute annually to this account – depending on your income from that year. For the current contribution amount allowed, go to the IRS website www.irs.gov/Retirement-Plans/. You can put the phrase "IRA Contribution" in the search box at the top of the webpage to locate the information. This is may be faster than trying to locate it by choosing "IRAs" under the "Topic for Retirement Plans" section in the column on the left, then choosing "Deduction Limits".

Money Market Account - regular savings or with checking privileges. This account normally requires a minimum balance to be maintained to qualify for a slightly higher interest payment, as compared to a standard savings account or free checking account.

The following list of 5 terms define the most common types of financial assets that the individual investor (you and me) will most likely buy in the course of our financial planning. I would also like to remind you that it is common practice for us to re-examine our accounts every 6 months and make changes according to our strategy and the behavior of the stock and bond markets.

Bonds – a financial instrument that is offered by an institution to raise funds for projects. Corporate and Municipal (Muni's) bonds are very common. When you buy a bond, you are considered a lender to the institution. They normally provide you with a monthly interest payment, or coupon. When they mature the institution pays you the original purchase value (principal). If the institution goes bankrupt, you can lose your money. You also may be familiar with the government bonds. You can purchase EE and I series savings bonds, T-bills, and other Treasuries from the U.S. government online at http://www.treasurydirect.gov/.

Money Market Fund – a mutual fund that invests in low risk, short term investments. Normally your cash balance in your brokerage account is invested in this type of fund for you. Your contributions, proceeds from stock sales, and dividends make up your cash balance. You use this money to purchase more stocks or transfer it back to you for spending elsewhere.

Mutual Funds – a group of stocks managed by a fund manager. Your investment is pooled together with other investors to increase the ownership opportunities in the stocks owned by the fund. These have an assortment of fees you need to be aware of.

Stock Shares – can be sold as a single unit, or in fractional units. Normally we, as individual investors, purchase them in single units. This is not a rule though, as some brokers purchase fractional units for you as well. You see this more with retirement accounts. The stock shares represent ownership interest in a company.

Treasuries – negotiable debt owned by our government. Common treasuries are treasury bonds, treasury bills, treasury notes, and treasury inflation protected securities (TIPS). As with the government bonds, you can also purchase treasuries directly from http://www.treasurydirect.gov/, or from a broker.

The next group of 8 terms is specific to dividend investors. These terms you will need to know to understand and monitor your investing goals and plan.

Declaration Date – the date the company directors announces the next dividend payment information.

Distribution – income generated from investments that are returned to investors. Normally a trust will distribute income to investors to avoid paying the taxes on the money. The investors pay the taxes. These are different from a dividend by the company, but are treated as income for you just the same.

Dividend / Special Dividends – profits that a company returns to the stock share owners on either a monthly, quarterly, or yearly basis. These are normally scheduled payments. Special dividends are not scheduled. These are paid whenever a company chooses to return more profit to the stock share owner in addition to the scheduled dividend payments.

Dividend Payout Ratio – the percentage of earnings a company pays to shareholders in the form of dividends.

Dividend Reinvestment Plan (DRIP) – a plan offered by some companies that will allow the dividend payment to be used to automatically purchase new stock shares, or fractions of stock shares, on the dividend payment date. I have noticed that the default setting on new accounts lean toward the automatic purchase of new shares of that company. You may need to have your broker change that setting to allow your dividends to accumulate in your cash balance instead, depending on your strategy.

Dividend Yield – the ratio a company provides that compares the amount of dividends paid out in relation to its share price over the span of 1 year. If a company pays out $1 and the average price of the stock share is $10, then the yield is 10%.

Ex-Dividend Date – this date is used to determine which owners can receive the next dividend. All of the stock shares purchased prior to the Ex-Dividend date should be eligible for the next dividend payment. Some stock purchases can take up to 3 business days before they are completed. You should always plan on buying stock at least 3 business days before the Ex-Dividend date if you want the next available dividend payment.

Payment Date – the date the dividend is actually paid to all of the stock share owners on record prior to the Ex-Dividend Date.

The next group of 4 terms describes the most common types of stock investment favored by dividend investors because of their higher dividend payout. These also normally involve more risk. I will discuss these more in depth in chapter 5.

Business Development Company (BDC) – they provide capital to small investors in compliance with Section 54 of the Investment Company Act of 1940. For more information on this act, see the report at this website: http://www.sec.gov/about/laws/ica40.pdf.
They are considered regulated investment companies (RIC) and therefore must distribute at least 90% of their profits to investors to maintain a special tax consideration. The small investors are normally considered somewhat risky in consideration of their ability to repay the loans. BDCs countermeasure this risk with other investments as best as possible.

Master Limited Partnership (MLP) – this is composed of two forms of partners, the first is the partner that manages the MLP. The second is the limited partner that provides capital for investment and receives periodic distribution payments. The MLP does not pay taxes from profit; the taxes are paid by the limited partners when they receive distributions. Common types of MLPs include crude oil/ refined petroleum pipeline owners, natural gas pipeline owners, propane distributors, and shipping operators. There are special tax rules to consider for these. More on that in chapter 6 (What About Taxes?).

Real Estate Investment Trust (REIT) – a type of security that sells like stock. It invests primarily in real estate property or mortgage activity. REIT's are considered regulated investment companies (RIC) and therefore must distribute at least 90% of their profits to investors to maintain a special tax consideration. A good website to use in your research of REITs is http://www.reit.com/.

Rural Telecoms – mostly known for providing landline telephone services (as opposed to wireless) and broadband internet to rural areas. They do not normally invest in research and development as they partner with other telephone companies to provide wireless cellular phone handsets and accessories, and are therefore able to pay higher dividends.

Lastly I will provide a short list (14) of some common stock market buzz words. You will undoubtedly run across more buzzwords or terms that you may not understand. I have provided 3 internet links in Appendix A to popular investment related online dictionaries.

Exchange Traded Fund (ETF) – a class of funds that trade (as opposed to individual stock). They have annual expenses and commission fees that you need to be aware of prior to purchasing any of these.

Index – a fake portfolio used as a comparison benchmark tool. You cannot invest in these. Standard & Poor's 500 (S & P 500) and the Dow Jones Industrial Average (DJIA) are very popular indexes used as a bench mark for other funds to compare against.

Insider Trading – the buy or sell of stocks by someone who has inside, or non-public, knowledge of the company and the related stock. This is illegal if the insiders makes the buy or sell before that knowledge is made public.

Margin – buying stocks using money borrowed from the brokerage firm. This is similar to taking a loan against assets you already own. A **"Margin Call"** is used when the value of the assets borrowed against drops, and you must immediately deposit cash to make up the difference.

Over The Counter (OTC) – are stocks that are sold by a dealer network as opposed to an exchange. Check with your brokerage firm to determine if they can broker the purchase of these stocks. Some trade on OTC Bulletin Boards (OTCBB). These are normally penny stocks or stocks of companies with bad credit.

Penny Stocks – some people refer to these as stocks that sell for less than $1. Other people consider any stock that sells off the market exchange, or OTC, as penny stocks.

Proxy – a legal document that allows one shareholder to authorize another shareholder to vote for them at the annual company meeting. As a stockholder, you will receive these proxy statements at least annually.

Portfolio – the collection of all of your investment assets.

Prospectus – a legal document that explains details about the investment to potential shareholders.

Return On Investment – the expected capital gain on an investment over a specific period of time. If you buy $1000 of a certain stock that distributes 7% in dividends annually, then you would expect to receive $70 on return.

SPDR – a group of Exchange Traded Funds that track the most common Indexes.

Stock Split / Reverse Split – a common practice where a company divides its common shares into more shares. If a company offers a two for one split (2:1), and you already owned 100 shares, you would then own 200 shares. This process does not increase your overall value of the shares you own. If the 100 shares were valued at $20 a share before the split, the 200 shares would be valued at $10 a share after the split. A reverse split is the opposite (1:2). Your 100 shares would then become 50.

Stock Symbol (ticker code) – a unique set of letters that identify a company being traded on the market. You will use these all the time.

Total Cost of Ownership – the complete cost includes stock share price, brokerage fee, and any other account fees. If you purchase $1000 of a certain stock and the broker fee was $60, and your account has an annual maintenance fee of $40, you add these together and divide by the number of shares you purchased. The result is the real cost per share that you paid.

CHAPTER 4

ACCOUNT MANAGEMENT

The more knowledgeable you are about your investments, the less likely you are to hand over all control of your money to someone else. The person who controls your money should be more concerned about the health and welfare of your money than the potential profits they can earn from fees charged to manage your money. To be fair, not all financial consultants and planners are only focused on their management fees. There are some very well trained and educated professionals who are actually concerned with the growth and stability of your funds entrusted to them.

In order to be successful you need to develop a strategy, set goals, and have a plan to execute, monitor, and modify that strategy as time goes on. I realize that there are some people who have no interest in managing their own money. Those people will most likely benefit mostly from the first account management option presented here.

Option 1: Give 100% control of your financial assets to a third party.

This third party will most likely be a licensed professional, such as a financial consultant or planner (remember FINRA from chapter 1?). This professional will most likely provide you with a risk assessment and recommend a blend of mutual funds that match that level of risk for your age group. **They make more money by selling you funds than by buying and selling you individual stock.** Please note that you can ask this professional to include funds that invest in dividend-paying stocks. Also make sure you are **FULLY** aware of all of the account related fees and fund related management fees that you will be paying. A normal fund management fee can be around 1% of your portfolio assets, divided up monthly. This would equate to about $100 divided by 12 months for a portfolio of $10,000, or $1000 dividend by 12 months for a portfolio of $100,000.

It is very important that you determine how that fee is collected. This management fee can be pulled from your assets in the account, as opposed to you receiving a bill in the mail. If you do not have enough in your account cash balance to pay this monthly fee, your professional will sell some assets to cover the fee costs. This can be expensive as you will not be earning any money on the assets that are sold. Funds also involve other fees such as load fees. These are charges or commissions paid by you when the fund is purchased or sold.

There is another type of financial professional who charges a flat fee for actual time spent managing your account (as opposed to the monthly management fee). The average hourly rate can be anywhere from $100 - $200. So if your professional meets with you once a year to review and make changes to your assets, it can cost you between $500 to $1000 depending on their hourly rate and the total time billed for their research and your onsite visit.

This deters the investor from meeting with the professional more than annually, which can be a big mistake as we need to review our assets at least every 6 months. I review mine at least every 3 months due to the volatile economy and stock market activity we have endured for the past 5 or 6 years. You may not need to review your account as often. You may choose to monitor the individual stocks weekly instead.

In some cases it would cost less to pay the hourly rate. If you have an extremely large portfolio, of say $500,000 or so, the hourly rate option may prove the better choice to save you money compared to the 1% option. You would pay that $500 - $1000 fee twice a year as opposed to $5,000 divided monthly for the first option.

From this example you can tell that it is imperative to know the fee structure your professional bills you with, and all other account related and fund related fees you will need to pay. Your individual situation will determine which option is best for you. Do not be afraid to do the math. It could be a very costly mistake not to compare both forms of fee structures.

Option 2: Give partial control of your financial assets to a third party, and manage the rest yourself.

This option may be helpful to control the amount of risk you take when you first start investing. Mutual funds are known to be less risky than individual stocks. This option involves owning both individual stocks and dividend stock funds. You can keep them in the same account or in separate accounts, whichever works best for you. The big difference with this option is that you will be choosing the individual stocks and funds to invest in, instead of your professional choosing for you. You will only be using the brokerage service, not the advisor and planner services.

You will pay the normal brokerage fees when you buy and sell the individual stocks and the normal fund management fees charged for mutual funds. The main purpose and goal for this strategy is to allow you to earn income from the funds while you learn which individual stock investments you want to make. Over time, you can sell the funds and use those earnings to purchase individual stocks.

About this time you may be wondering other then the fees, what else is the big difference between owning funds or individual stocks? The answer to that involves controlling risk (of losing your money). Brokerage account investments are not protected by the Federal Deposit Insurance Corporation (http://www.fdic.gov/). Because of this, we have the risk of losing our capital investment (money).

This is where risk management comes in. The higher the risk of the investment the higher the risk of you losing money. Your choices concerning which stock to purchase should reflect your current level of acceptable risk (high, medium, or low). I am good with accepting more risk than my spouse is. I am a medium-high risk taker (specific to investing money), and my spouse is medium-low. I treat our retirement accounts with his medium-low risk and our non-retirement brokerage account with my medium-high risk attitude.

Mutual funds are considered lower risk as they contain many individual stocks. The chance that all of the stocks in the fund losing a large amount of value are relatively small. The risk involved in buying individual stocks is greater as that risk is based completely on that one company that issued the stock shares. In addition to this, the market industry considers high paying dividend stocks to be more risky than lower paying dividend, or no paying dividend stocks. To help reduce some of the risk associated with high paying dividend stocks, some monitoring of the company's financial health is needed. This is where we learn to use the free online resources located in Appendix A.

Online Stock Screeners help us to search for potential stocks to review for our strategy. The dividend and stock monitoring news sites provide free analyst ratings and comments from investment professionals. You should be able to find up to date information on the company available cash flow, which is needed to pay dividends, and their overall health compared to other similar companies. The news also lets you know when the markets are down, so you can check your target stock prices and determine if they are low enough to buy.

Option 3: Manage 100% of your financial assets yourself.

This option involves you performing all of the research and decisions concerning what individual high paying dividend stock purchases you want to make. You can also lower your brokerage fees by choosing to issue the buy and sell transactions using the online investment tools provided by a handful of online investment firms that cater to the do it yourself investing crowd. If you are computer savvy, then this option could be for you.

For this option to succeed, you need to plan your investing education. The learning curve here involves using the free online investment tools training guides and tutorials, and using the free online stock screeners and analyst reports to choose your dividend stocks. I have looked at the top 3 online investment firms websites and reviewed the tools they provide for you to manage your accounts. They seem to be well written and offer customer service help if you have questions. In Appendix A, I provide 3 internet links to brokerage review sites.

What I found is that you will save money by paying reduced broker fees, starting at $7 for one of the firms. I called the local office for that firm and asked a few questions. The $7 fee is good for individual stocks that you submit the buy or sell order through the online tool. If you call the office to submit an order, the fee will be around $32. The broker in the office has to make money too. You can purchase funds directly from the tool also, but the fee is different as the "load" commission fees also come into play here.

You can also fund your account online by adding your local checking account to your profile. This can take a few days to get verified, depending on the bank. If you want to go to a local office for the brokerage firm (if there is one in your area), they can open your account and accept a check to fund it. Please note that these brokerage firms require a minimum initial deposit. The one I talked to had a minimum deposit of $500.

Note: If you transfer account funds from one investment firm/ broker to another, you will have to pay transfer fees. I have seen some of the firms offering a reimbursement of up to $100 of the fees you owe the previous firm. You may also have to pay sell and buy brokerage/ fund fees during this process.

CHAPTER 5

SET GOALS, MAKE A PLAN

For your financial investing strategy to succeed, you must set realistic goals and have a plan to execute to reach those goals. A goal is a specific result that you want to achieve. You determine the goal and you make a plan on how to reach or achieve that goal. A goal needs to be something that you can actually reach. Too many times people set unrealistic or impossible goals. When they fail to reach that goal, they get disappointed and give up.

In the financial world, I try to set new goals for each year. To me this is manageable. I generally know how much money I can invest in the upcoming year, and I generally know how much return I can expect on my investment for that year. Normally my goal is a response to a purpose, or a reason I have chosen to invest. The plan is used to reach that goal to satisfy my purpose. Your purpose could be to generate monthly income to supplement your other income. Your purpose could also be to build up your account using both the dividends and cash you add to purchase more stock. Whatever your purpose is, it is necessary to determine if dividend stock investing is the right tool to successfully reach your defined goals to satisfy your purpose.

Let us look at an example of setting a goal. We will use the example of our purpose, or desire, to generate as much cash as we can to supplement our monthly income now. We would need to identify how much money we require each month to be generated by the investment account. For this example we will say that we need to generate an additional $50 a month, on average.

To achieve this goal, we will need to determine what investment strategy to use in our plan. We will follow our plan to reach the goal ($50 a month income).

First we will need to identify how much cash we need to invest to reach this goal. We can identify that by choosing one of the higher dividend paying stocks. For this example we choose a fictional stock "abc". This stock provides a 10% dividend monthly. So we would need 500 shares of this stock to get $50 a month. (500 shares x .10 = $50). That does not sound too bad so far. We will say that the "abc" stock is currently selling for $8 a share. That means that we would expect to need at least $4000 (500 shares x $8 = $4000) to invest in a monthly paying dividend stock to get the $50.

The example sounds good and simple until we add some additional information. If you chose account management option 3 from the previous chapter and created you own online account and issue the buy transaction order for the 500 shares of "abc" company, it could cost you as low as $7. Provided that there is no account maintenance fee and your buy order is completed when the "abc" stock is actually at $8 a share, then your total cost is $4007. Keep in mind that stock prices fluctuate continuously throughout the day. You may issue the buy transaction at $8, but the actual price may be $8.10 when the transaction completes. It may also be $7.90. Just make sure that you have enough cash balance in your account to cover this possible variance.

Another variance for this example is the potential for "abc" company to change the dividend. Companies can change their dividends for a couple of reasons. One reason is that they want to use the available cash to pay down debt. This is a good thing even though they cut your dividend. Another reason is that they did not generate enough cash profit in the previous quarter to pay the same dividend. In our example "abc" paid out a dividend of 10%. If they cut it to 8%, our payout would decrease to 500 shares x .08 = $40. So we would need to modify our plan and purchase more shares. We would need an additional 150 shares to return to the $50 monthly payout (650 x .08 = $50).

I am now going to bump up the math from the previous example and provide you with current real examples from Real Estate Investment Trusts (REITs), Business Development Companies (BDCs), Master Limited Partnerships (MLPs), and Rural Telecoms. To maintain my unbiased state, I am not providing the real stock ticker, but you will easily find them on any stock screener, or email me at Finance@weblori.com for them:

REIT 1 - currently pays monthly dividend at around 17%. Stock price today is around $6.75. The dividend for March, 2013 is .08 / share. In order for you to get $50 a month for this stock, you would need 625 shares ($50 / .08 = 625). If we round up the stock price to $7, you would need an investment of approximately $4375, plus the $7 online broker fee.

REIT 2 – currently pays quarterly dividends (Jan, April, July, and Oct) at just over 13%. Stock price today is around $15.30. The dividend for April is .45 / share. In order to get your $150 each quarter, you would need around 334 shares ($150 / .45 = 333.3333). If we round up the stock price to $15.50, you would need an investment of approximately $5177, plus the $7 online broker fee.

BDC 1 – currently pays monthly dividends at around 11%. Stock price today is around $11.25. The dividend for March is .1101 / share. In order for you to get $50 a month for this stock, you would need 455 shares ($50 / .1101 = 454.1326). If we round the up the stock price to $11.50, you would need an investment of approximately $5232.50, plus the $7 online broker fee.

BDC 2 - currently pays monthly dividends at around 10%. Stock price today is around $11.00. The dividend for March is .0958 / share. In order for you to get $50 a month for this stock, you would need 522 shares ($50 / .0958 = 521.9206). If we round the up the stock price to $11.25, you would need an investment of approximately $5872.50, plus the $7 online broker fee.

MLP 1 - currently pays quarterly dividends (Feb, May, Aug, and Nov) at just over 8%. Stock price today is around $26.50. The dividend for Feb was .57 / share. In order to get your $150 each quarter, you would need around 264 shares ($150 / .57 = 263.1578). If we round up the stock price to $26.75, you would need an investment of approximately $7062, plus the $7 online broker fee.

MLP 2 - currently pays quarterly dividends (Feb, May, Aug, and Nov) at just over 7%. Stock price today is around $37.75. The dividend for Feb was .725 / share. In order to get your $150 each quarter, you would need around 207 shares ($150 / .725 = 206.8965). If we round up the stock price to $38.00, you would need an investment of approximately $7866, plus the $7 online broker fee.

Rural Telecom 1 - currently pays quarterly dividends (March, June, Sept, and Dec) at just over 9.5%. Stock price today is around $4.25. The dividend for March is .10 / share. In order to get your $150 each quarter, you would need around 1500 shares ($150 / .10 = 1500). If we round up the stock price to $4.50, you would need an investment of approximately $6750, plus the $7 online broker fee.

Rural Telecom 2 - currently pays quarterly dividends (March, June, Sept, and Dec) at just over 11%. Stock price today is around $8.60. The dividend for March is .25 / share. In order to get your $150 each quarter, you would need around 600 shares ($150 / .25 = 600). If we round up the stock price to $8.75, you would need an investment of approximately $5250, plus the $7 online broker fee.

I think you can see from the above real life examples that in order to get the goal of at least $50 each month in dividend payouts, you will need an investment of at least $4375 to as high as $7866 (plus $7 online broker fee).

You may also have noticed that not all of the stocks pay monthly dividends, in fact most pay quarterly. My personal plan involved selling my regular growth stock (I had been buying these since 2003) that did not pay dividends and purchasing stock that did. I had to come up with a plan to determine which new stocks to buy and goals on how much of each of the new stocks I needed to satisfy my purpose. Of course my plan had to be complex and involved more than 1 phase. Here is what I actually did:

It all started about 10 years ago I decided that I wanted to learn how to make money investing in the stock market. I saved money and purchased growth stocks. These are the kinds that increase in the value of their share price instead of paying a dividend. I both lost and gained some money.

Finally, about 3 years ago I decided to change my investment strategy. Due to the weakening job market, I decided that I wanted to create a way to generate extra money every month in the event that either I or my spouse lost our jobs. So my purpose changed from wanting to learn how to make money buying and selling stocks, to wanting to make an investment that would generate monthly income.

In my first phase I set my first goal. It was to achieve a monthly dividend of any amount. I started by purchasing MLP 2 with funds I received from selling oil and gas stock I owned. Well, that took care of 4 months. My next sell of financial stocks gave me enough to purchase Rural Telecom 1 which paid in a different set of 4 months. So that took care of 8 months. My final sell of the financial stocks gave me enough funds to purchase a REIT 2 that paid quarterly dividends in the remaining 4 months. So after about 1 year of re-design, I now was receiving some kind of dividends every month of the year.

My next phase of my plan was to set a minimum monthly dividend amount goal. At this time, I was receiving dividends, but they were different from month to month. I wanted to get them to be close to the same. So for the next several months I saved the dividends in my cash account and continued to contribute extra funds to that account. That plan allowed me to purchase enough extra shares of each stock to get to my baseline goal.

My final phase involved extensive research on monthly paying dividends. I found that Canada has some very good paying oil and gas related stocks, but I did not want to look into the tax implications at that time. I instead chose REIT 1. I then set a goal for the total amount of shares I wanted for this stock. As REIT 1 is a monthly paying stock, all dividend amounts for each month of the year increased at the same level. When I purchased enough of that stock, I started planning on BDC 2. I set a new goal and reached that goal in 8 months. Currently I am working on my new goal that I set for the purchase of BDC 1.

REITs, BDCs, MLPS, and Rural Telecoms are considered very risky investments to some people. Each category has its own risk. The higher the dividend percentage, the higher the risk is in most cases. Part of my research of these stock companies concluded that the analyst reports are mostly accurate for at least 12 months out. So an analyst will look at the previous 4th quarter company results and forward planning for the new year, and determine the ability for that company to be able to pay the upcoming dividends for the current year.

So now you may be thinking about REIT 1 and are asking yourself "where do I get that initial $4375 to buy the stock that will pay me $50 a month"? If you do not already have this cash hanging out in your wallet, you will need to make a plan to save it. Provided that you have the initial minimum deposit of $500 to open your investment account, you will need to decide how much you can set aside each month to build up to the remaining $3875. You may need to have a long term plan to put whatever money you can set aside into the account, and purchase stock each time you have reached a goal.

Your goal can be to purchase stock each time you reach $200 in your cash account. This way you will slowly build up the number of shares, and earn some dividends, while you work toward your final goal of owning 500 shares. Some people use their income tax returns to expedite the time to reach their final goal. Other people may find a temporary job to help generate the needed cash. Still others may give up something they pay for each month to get the extra cash.

The important thing to remember is that you need to set realistic goals that you can actually have a chance to reach, and then create a plan to execute to get you there. Remember also that things have a bad habit of changing on us. The stock prices change all the time. The dividend payout may get cut, or it can get an increase. You will need to monitor your plan and adjust your goals in response to this change. Always expect that change will happen.

Because change does happen, I like to monitor my target stock price (the next stock I am going to buy) and wait until the price goes on sale. This can happen when our target company has bad news, another company in the same "sector" has bad news, or our current state of the economy or politics give us the **PERCEPTION** of bad news in the media.

I used the word perception as politics and emotions should not control the overall value of the stocks on the market, but we see everyday where it does. If you read that the Federal Reserve is going to make a statement tomorrow, you will see the price of shares of stock drop today. This is part of the fear factor. Investors (normally fund managers, not individuals) will be concerned that the Fed Chairman will tell us bad news and those investors may sell some or all of their government treasuries. The weird thing is that this affects other sectors of the market as well.

As an individual investor, I wait for these times as I consider the stock market to be "on sale". It is always a fun challenge to try to time your buy order when you think the stock prices are at a low. Before the 2007 recession set everything off balance in the markets, you could almost always count on March and December as good times to buy. Historically March was the month when the markets made a "correction". I am not an economist, but I believe this is due to the companies having provided their previous year end results to the public. These results would identify the current true value of the company and its stock shares.

The end of December was always another good time for the market to drop. Post 2007, we see major fluctuations on a monthly basis. Due to this negative effect on the market, I find myself monitoring my target stock share price almost on a daily basis. There are wonderful free tools that will help you do this. Use as many tools as you can to help manage the amount of time you spend on research and decision making in support of your plan.

Here are 2 examples of some filters you can screen for when locating high paying dividend stocks. You can use the free stock screener links provided in appendix A for this.

This filter returned 59 companies on finviz.com:

Dividend Yield greater than 7%

Return On Assets = positive

Debt/EQ is less than 0.5

Country = USA

This filter returned 24 companies on finviz.com:

Dividend Yield greater than 10%

Return On Assets = positive

Debt/EQ is less than 0.5

Country = USA

Note: This is also a good time to mention that some companies offer the Dividend Reinvestment Plan (DRIP) as described in chapter 3. I have noticed that some of the brokerage firms have this setting as default. Meaning that if your target stock company participates in this plan; your dividends may automatically be reinvested to buy more shares, as opposed to landing as available cash in your account. If this is not part of your plan, please make sure you check that this setting is not the default on your account.

Note2: My personal plan, as described in the previous pages, provides an example of compounding dividends. I take the dividends I get paid and purchase more shares with them, further increasing my monthly dividend payout. At any time, I can start taking the monthly dividend payments back in cash if I need to. I can also sell the stock for cash or re-invest in another stock.

CHAPTER 6

WHAT ABOUT TAXES?

Yes, we must pay taxes on our capital gains, dividends, interest, and distributions earned in our non-retirement plan brokerage account. I mention this as retirement accounts can also have brokerage services, and the taxes are treated differently. This chapter will review the different tax considerations and expectations as painlessly as possible.

1. When you sell a stock, you will either earn money or lose money in this transaction. If you earn money, this is considered "Capital Gain" for the purpose of your income tax reporting. If you lose money, this is considered "Capital Loss". You must pay taxes on the "Capital Gain". You can also report "Capital Loss" on your income taxes to reduce your overall taxes owed.

2. You should receive a 1099 form from your brokerage firm that provides the information you need to report your taxable income when preparing your annual income tax forms. There is more than one type of 1099 form. The 1099-DIV is used for dividends and distributions. The 1099-INT is used for Interest earned on the cash portion of your account. The 1099-B is used to list your capital gains and losses. You can receive one 1099 form with all of these included. It is commonly called the 1099-enhanced form.

3. Some Municipal Bonds have yields that are tax free. Know your "munis" tax status.

4. If you maintain ownership of a stock transaction for more than 1 year, this is considered "Long Term". When you sell that stock and earn a gain, this is considered 'Long Term Capital Gain". It is taxed LOWER than "Short Term", or less than 1 year ownership of stock.

5. Master Limited Partnership (MLP) offers a tax-deferred distribution as opposed to a normal dividend. What this means is that the unit (share) holder will a special tax document in February or March called the K-1. This document will specify how much of your distributions are tax deferred. You pay the taxes when you sell the unit (share). The Internal Revenue Service (IRS) has a form to help us understand our tax responsibility. It is the IRS Publication Form 1065. You use the information from the K-1 form sent to you by the MLP to fill out the worksheet on IRS Publication 1065. Tax software programs allow you to enter K-1 information under the "Other Income" Category.

In the past (pre-2013) we have paid about 15% tax on these forms of income. As part of the Affordable Care Act of 2010, there has been added a Net Investment Tax (NIT) that took effect on Jan 1st, 2013. This new tax adds 3.8% to the pre-existing 15% for those individuals, estates, and trusts that have investment income and modified adjusted gross income over the following:

Married filing separately	$125,000
Single or Head of Household	$200,000
Qualifying widow	$250,000
Married filing jointly	$250,000

More on this can be found here:

http://www.irs.gov/uac/Newsroom/Net-Investment-Income-Tax-FAQs.

More on other Affordable Care Act provisions can be found here:

http://www.irs.gov/uac/Affordable-Care-Act-Tax-Provisions

Lastly, if you own Canadian stocks and are a resident of the U.S., there is a treaty between the U.S. and Canada specific to claiming income tax on dividends and distributions. The purpose was to avoid paying taxes to both countries on the same income. The treaty is covered under IRS publication 597 located here:

U.S. and Canada Income Tax Treaty - publication 597 (09/2011):
http://www.irs.gov/publications/p597/index.html

If you need information concerning income tax status for Canada, the link is here: www.cra-arc.gc.ca. The Canadian Non-Resident (NR) form most commonly used to declare income is:

NR301 - Declaration of Eligibility for Benefits under a Tax Treaty for a Non-Resident Taxpayer.

APPENDIX A

USEFUL ONLINE RESOURCES

(Note: some of the resources are free depending on how much you use them. You should not have to create a logon account to use these. The links provided are good as of February 2013, if the link does not appear to work when you try it – try to use the top-level domain i.e.: www.finviz.com etc..)

Free online stock screeners:

1. http://finviz.com/screener.ashx
2. http://www.marketwatch.com/tools/stockresearch/screener/
3. http://screener.finance.yahoo.com/stocks.html

Free investing related personal education:

1. http://money.cnn.com/magazines/moneymag/money101/
2. http://www.money.cnn.com/retirement/guide/
3. http://www.finra.org/Investors/index.htm

Free online investment terms definitions:

1. http://www.investopedia.com/
2. http://www.investorwords.com/
3. http://www.morningstar.com/InvGlossary/

Free dividend monitoring site:

1. http://www.dividendinvestor.com/

2. http://dividata.com/

3. Stock specific corporate website, "Investor Relations"

Free stock market news and monitoring sites:

1. http://www.morningstar.com/

2. http://www.fool.com/

3. http://seekingalpha.com/

Free brokerage firm review sites:

1. http://www.brokerage-review.com/stock-brokers/top-5-brokerages.aspx

2. http://www.stockbrokers.com/onlinestockbrokers.html

3. http://www.smartmoney.com/invest/stocks/

Note: These free online resources can change from time to time. For current internet resource links, please check the financial page on my website: www.WebLori.com.

ABOUT THE AUTHOR

Lori O'Dette-Robinson is the owner and webmaster of the www.WebLori.com website. She is from Northern New York but now lives in Central Arkansas. She has served 6 years in the U.S. Army/Reserves. She has over 19 years experience in the Information Security and Application support fields for both the Mainframe and Client/Server environments.

She has her Master of Science degree in Information Security and Assurance. She is currently employed full time as a MTS IV Consultant-System Engineering with a Fortune 50 telecommunications company. She currently holds several industry standard professional certifications including the CISSP and GIAC G2700.

In her spare time, she has also been independently researching financial investments for more than 10 years and has developed a strong stock dividend portfolio. During this time she has acquired hundreds of hours of research concerning every aspect of money management, starting from the basic to advanced level understanding of different forms of currencies, the flow of money through our system, debt, credit, investment, and retirement strategies.

www.ingramcontent.com/pod-product-compliance
Lightning Source LLC
Chambersburg PA
CBHW051427200326
41520CB00023B/7387